Contents

What you need to know about the National Tests

Preparing and practising for the Maths Test

Instructions	1
Test A (Levels 3–5)	2
Test B (Levels 3–5)	16
Test C (Level 6)	30
Mental Arithmetic	37
Answers	38
Mental Arithmetic Questions	55
Determining your child's level	57
Marking Grid	58

What you need to know about the National Tests

KEY STAGE 2 NATIONAL TESTS: HOW THEY WORK

Pupils between the ages of 7 and 11 (Years 3–6) cover Key Stage 2 of the National Curriculum. In May of their final year of Key Stage 2 (Year 6), all pupils take written National Tests (commonly known as SATs) in English, Mathematics and Science. The tests are carried out in school, under the supervision of teachers, but are marked by examiners outside the school.

The tests help to show what children have learned in these key subjects. They also help parents and teachers to know whether children are reaching the standards set out in the National Curriculum.

Each child will probably spend around five hours in total sitting the tests during one week in May. Most children will do two papers in Mathematics and Science, and three in English.

The school will send the papers away to external examiners for marking. The school will then report the results of the tests to you by the end of July, along with the results of assessments made by teachers in the classroom, based on your child's work throughout Key Stage 2. You will also receive a summary of the results for all pupils at the school, and for pupils nationally. This will help you to compare the performance of your child with that of other children of the same age. The report from your child's school will explain to you what the results show about your child's progress, strengths, particular achievements and targets for development. It may also explain how to follow up the results with your child's teachers.

In addition, the publication of primary school performance (or 'league') tables will show how your child's school has performed in the teacher assessments and tests, compared to other schools locally and nationally.

UNDERSTANDING YOUR CHILD'S LEVEL OF ACHIEVEMENT

The National Curriculum divides standards for performance in each subject into a number of levels, from one to eight. On average, children are expected to advance one level for every two years they are at school. By Year 6 (the end of Key Stage 2), your child should be at Level 4. The table on page iii shows how your child is expected to progress through the levels at ages 7, 11 and 14 (the end of Key Stages 1, 2 and 3).

Most children will take the two papers for Levels 3–5 in Maths. One paper will allow the use of a calculator, and one will ban the use of a calculator. The two papers will contain the same number of marks. Each paper will be 45 minutes long. Your child may also take a mental arithmetic test as part of a national pilot in 1997, although the results of this pilot will not affect your child's overall level in Maths. Extension papers with Level 6 questions are available for exceptionally able pupils.

What you need to know about the National Tests

- ☐ Exceptional performance
- ■ Exceeded targets for age group
- ☐ Achieved targets for age group
- ■ Working towards targets for age group

How your child should progress

This book concentrates on Levels 3–5, giving plenty of practice to help your child achieve the best level possible. There are also some Level 6 questions for very able pupils. Do not worry if your child cannot do these questions; remember that Level 4 is the target level for children at the end of Key Stage 2. The bar chart below shows you what percentage of pupils nationally reached each of the levels in the 1996 tests for Maths.

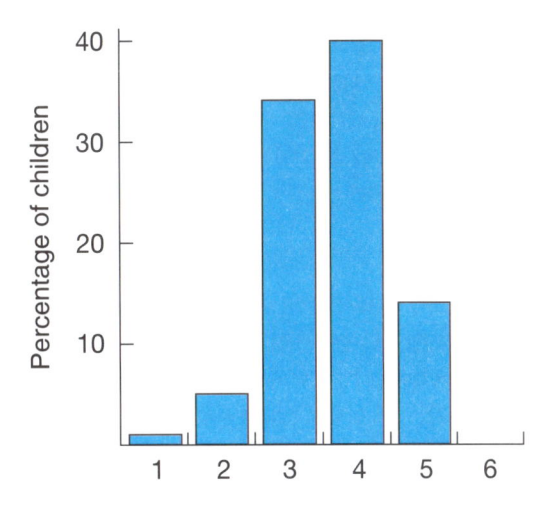

Levels achieved in Mathematics, 1996

Although the results of all reading, spelling and mathematics tests will be reported in terms of a subject level, these test scores will also be converted into an age-standardised score, to show the school how your child's score in these tests compares with that of his or her age group.

iii

Preparing and practising for the Maths Test

MATHS AT KEY STAGE 2
The questions in this book will test your child on the Key Stage 2 curriculum for Mathematics. For assessment purposes, the National Curriculum divides Mathematics into four sections, called Attainment Targets (ATs). The first AT, Using and Applying Mathematics, is assessed only by the teacher in the classroom, not in the written tests. The other three ATs are:
- AT2: Number
- AT3: Shape, Space and Measures
- AT4: Handling Data

The National Curriculum describes levels of performance for each of the four Mathematics ATs. These AT levels are taken together to give an overall level for Mathematics. The test papers have questions covering ATs 2–4. National Test questions are designed to assess your child's ability in four areas:
- Knowledge and understanding
- Handling information
- Interpretation and evaluation
- Problem solving

The questions in this book cover these skills.

USING THIS BOOK TO HELP YOUR CHILD PREPARE
This book contains four basic features:

Questions:	one non-calculator and one calculator test paper for Levels 3–5, one extension paper for Level 6 and one (optional) mental arithmetic test
Answers:	showing acceptable responses and marks
Notes to Parent:	giving advice on how to help your child avoid common mistakes and improve his or her score
Level Charts:	showing you how to interpret your child's marks to arrive at a level for each test and overall

SETTING THE TESTS AT HOME
Try setting Test A first, mark it to see how your child has done and work through the answers and advice together. Then set Test B on a different day. Let your child carry out the tests in a place where he or she is comfortable. Your child will need the equipment listed on page vi. In your own words, describe to your child how to work through the test. Make sure to work through the instructions on page 1 together.

Note the starting time in the box at the top of each test. During the test, if your child cannot read a word you may read it out. If he or she does not understand a word, you can explain what the word means, providing it is not a mathematical word. For example, you can explain what is meant by the word 'conversion' but not 'quadrilateral' or 'decimal'.

Preparing and practising for the Maths Test

After 45 minutes, ask your child to stop writing. If he or she has not finished, but wishes to continue working on the test, draw a line to show how much has been completed within the test time. Then let your child work to the end of the test, but check that he or she is able to cope with the questions as they generally become more difficult.

Test C is an Extension Paper, designed for exceptionally able children. Your child should attempt Test C only if the results of Tests A and B suggest that he or she is working at Level 5 or higher. Test C should take 30 minutes and a calculator may be used.

MARKING THE QUESTIONS

When your child has completed a test, turn to the Answers section at the back of the book. Work through the answers with your child, using the Notes to Parent to help give advice, correct mistakes and explain problems. If your child required extra time to complete a test, go through all the questions with your child, but do not include the marks for the 'extra' questions in the total scores.

Using the recommended answers, award your child the appropriate mark or marks for each question. In the margin of each test page, there are small boxes divided in half. The marks available for each question are at the bottom; write your child's score in the top half of the box.

Enter the total number of marks for each question on the Marking Grid on page 58. Then add them up to find the total for the test. Look at the Level Charts on page 57 to determine your child's level for each test, as well as an overall level.

ABOUT THE MENTAL ARITHMETIC TEST

Mental arithmetic is becoming an increasingly important part of the National Curriculum. In 1997, a mental arithmetic test will be introduced as a national pilot in which all schools may participate. The results of this pilot will help to determine the exact nature of the test when it becomes compulsory in 1998. As with the national pilot, the mental arithmetic test in this book is optional and will not contribute to your child's overall level in Mathematics. However, you may wish to use this test as extra practice, and to prepare your child for the types of question he or she may encounter in the pilot test.

Preparing and practising for the Maths Test

EQUIPMENT YOUR CHILD WILL NEED
The following equipment may be needed for answering these questions:
- a pen, pencil and rubber
- a ruler (30 cm plastic ruler is most suitable)
- a calculator. An inexpensive four-function calculator is all that is required. Do not let your child use a scientific calculator which has too many complicated functions.

- Angle measurer
  The angle measurer is probably easier to use than the protractor, particularly for angles greater than 180°.

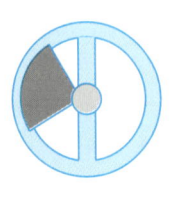

- Tracing paper
  This is useful for rotational symmetry questions.

- A pair of compasses
  Use this for drawing circles.

- A mirror
  This is useful for symmetry questions.

FINALLY, AS THE TESTS DRAW NEAR
In the days before the tests, make sure your child is as relaxed and confident as possible. You can help by:

- ensuring your child knows what test papers he or she will be doing;
- working through practice questions, and discussing which answers are right and why;
- checking that your child has all the relevant equipment.

Although the National Tests are important, your child's achievement throughout the school year is equally important. Encourage your child to do his or her best without putting him or her under too much pressure. Many children look forward to tests, but it is natural that some may be nervous. Look out for signs of anxiety, such as changes in eating or sleeping habits, and reassure your child if he or she is worried about these tests.

Instructions

Tests A and B should each take about 45 minutes.

Read all the words carefully. Look at any diagrams or pictures which should help you.

The questions for you to answer are in blue boxes.

For example:

Write down the next two numbers in the pattern.

Look for the ✏️➢ to show you where to write your answer.

Remember to show your working if you are asked to do so.

After finishing a page, turn over to a new page without waiting to be told.

If a question is too hard, you should move on to the next question.

You may not use a calculator in Test A, but you may use a calculator in Test B.

GOOD LUCK!

TEST A
LEVELS 3-5

MARKS

WITHOUT CALCULATOR

Test A

Start ☐ Finish ☐

1   On a village club cricket score board there are hooks for the scorer to hang number cards.

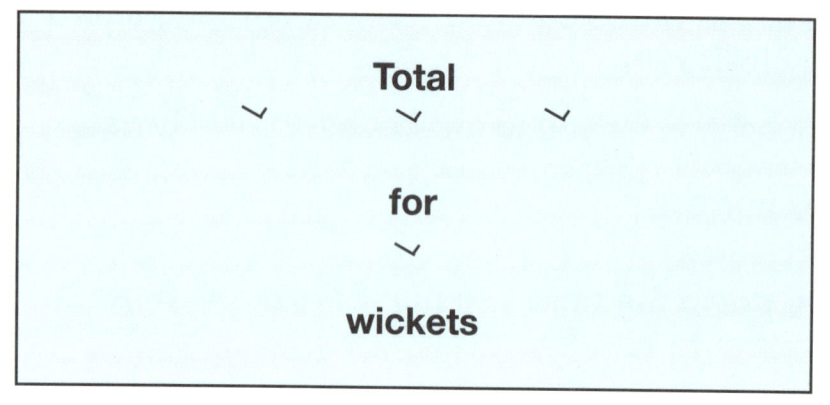

```
        Total
   ˅     ˅      ˅

         for
          ˅

       wickets
```

Using only these three number cards

[2] [4] [1]

one total he can make is:

[2] [4] [1]

a   **What is the smallest number he can make using all three cards?**

[ ] [ ] [ ]

b   **Make TWO numbers which are greater than 241.**

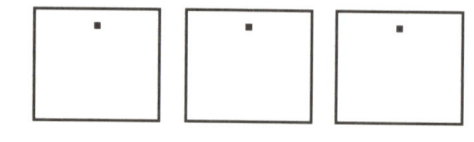

(i) [ ] [ ] [ ]

(ii) [ ] [ ] [ ]

1 Q1a

2 Q1b

2

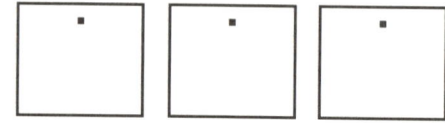

Test A

2   You may use a mirror or tracing paper to help you with this question.
Shapes can be symmetrical or not symmetrical.

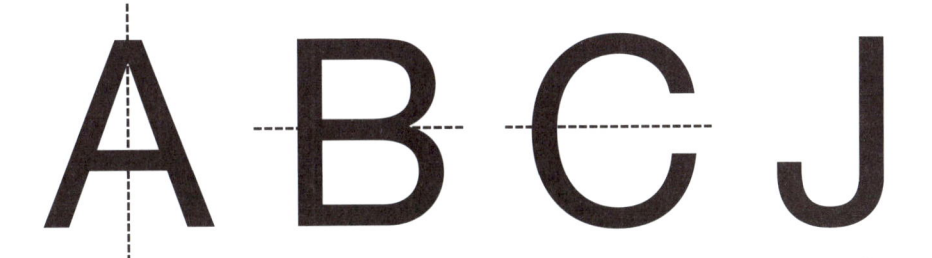

A B C J

------------------------------ is a mirror line.

A, **B** and **C** are symmetrical.
J is not symmetrical.

Look at the shapes **E**, **F**, **G** and **H**.

a   **Which letters are symmetrical?**

E F G H

b   **Draw one mirror line on each shape that is symmetrical.**

3   This chart shows the results of a traffic survey of the vehicles which passed the school gates each lunchtime during one week.

	Monday	Tuesday	Wednesday	Thursday	Friday
Cars	6	8	6	6	7
Lorries	2	1	0	3	3
Buses	2	0	3	5	1
Motorbikes	0	1	1	2	0
Tankers	1	1	0	2	1
Vans	2	3	2	1	2
Bicycles	4	6	5	4	2

a How many vehicles altogether passed on Tuesday lunchtime?

.... vehicles

b How many lorries passed during the week?

.... lorries

Test A

Here is a graph showing the number of each type of vehicle which passed on Thursday lunchtime.

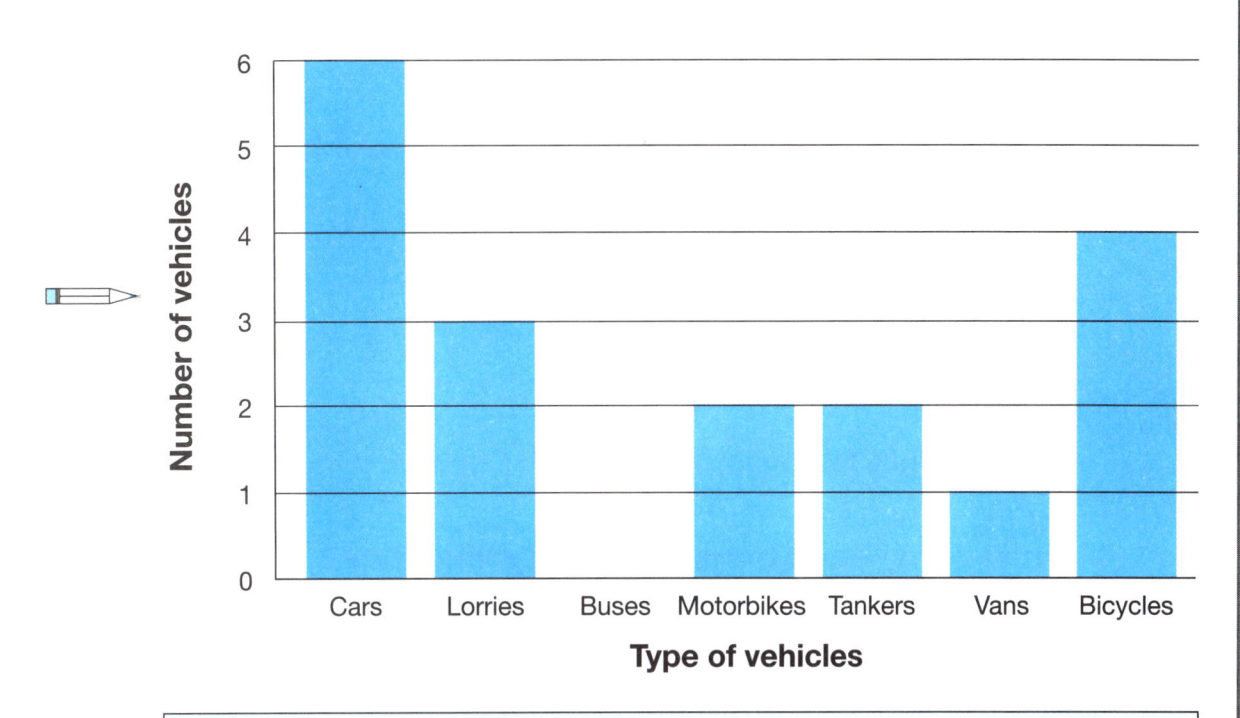

Number of vehicles (bar chart):
- Cars: 6
- Lorries: 3
- Buses: (missing)
- Motorbikes: 2
- Tankers: 2
- Vans: 1
- Bicycles: 4

Type of vehicles

c Draw in the missing column for the buses using the data from the chart.

d The pictogram below shows the number of cars which passed during the week.

🚗 = 2 cars

Finish the pictogram.

Monday	🚗 🚗 🚗
Tuesday	🚗 🚗 🚗 🚗
Wednesday	🚗 🚗 🚗
Thursday	
Friday	

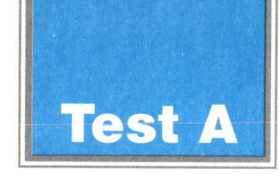

4 Helen collects the eggs from her hens.
She collects 40 eggs.
She wants to put them into boxes of six.

a **Work out how many boxes she will need.
Show your working.**

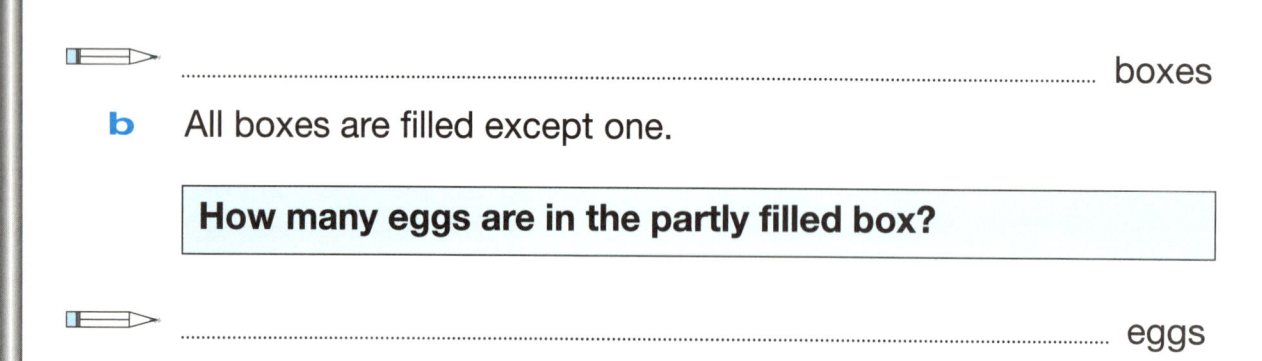

.... boxes

b All boxes are filled except one.

How many eggs are in the partly filled box?

.... eggs

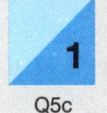

Test A

5 You are given these number sentences:

216 × 60 = 12960   6480 × 2 = 12960

Use this information to find the value of the following:

a   216 × 59

(You must show your working.)

b   432 × 60

(You must show your working.)

c $\dfrac{12960}{216}$ = ☐

d   216 × ☐ = 6480

TEST A
LEVELS 3–5

MARKS

Test A

6   A survey was carried out to show the popularity of television programmes in 1995 and 1996.
The pie charts below display the results.

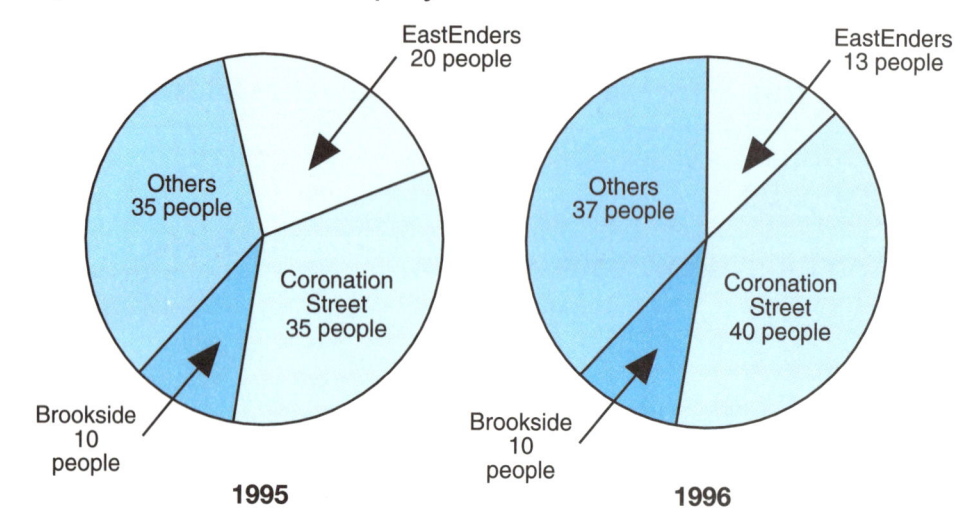

1995 pie chart: EastEnders 20 people, Others 35 people, Coronation Street 35 people, Brookside 10 people.

1996 pie chart: EastEnders 13 people, Others 37 people, Coronation Street 40 people, Brookside 10 people.

(*Programmes included in 'others' had fewer than 10 people voting for them.*)

a   **How many people took part in the survey each year?**

b   **Which was the most popular programme with the people asked in 1996?**

c   **Which programme had the same popularity in the two surveys?**

d   **Which programme was less popular in 1996 than 1995?**

e   **Suggest ONE way in which a survey of this type could be made more reliable.**

1 Q6a
1 Q6b
1 Q6c
1 Q6d
1 Q6e

8

7 You may use tracing paper for this question. This question is about shapes seen in the centre of car wheels.

This wheel will look the same after a quarter turn. In one complete turn it will look the same in *four* different positions.

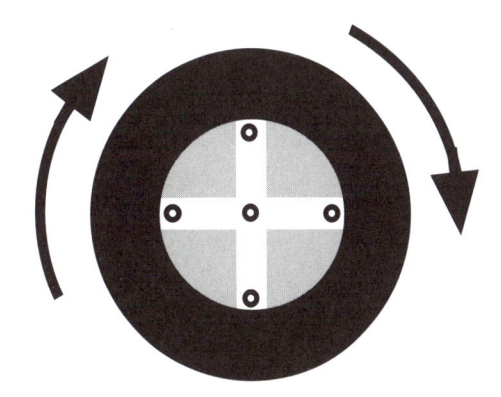

This wheel will only look the same after one complete turn. It will look the same in only *one* position.

In how many positions during one complete turn will these four wheels look the same?

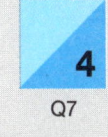

a

b

c

d

8 On this grid draw a six-sided shape which has three pairs of parallel sides and reflective symmetry.

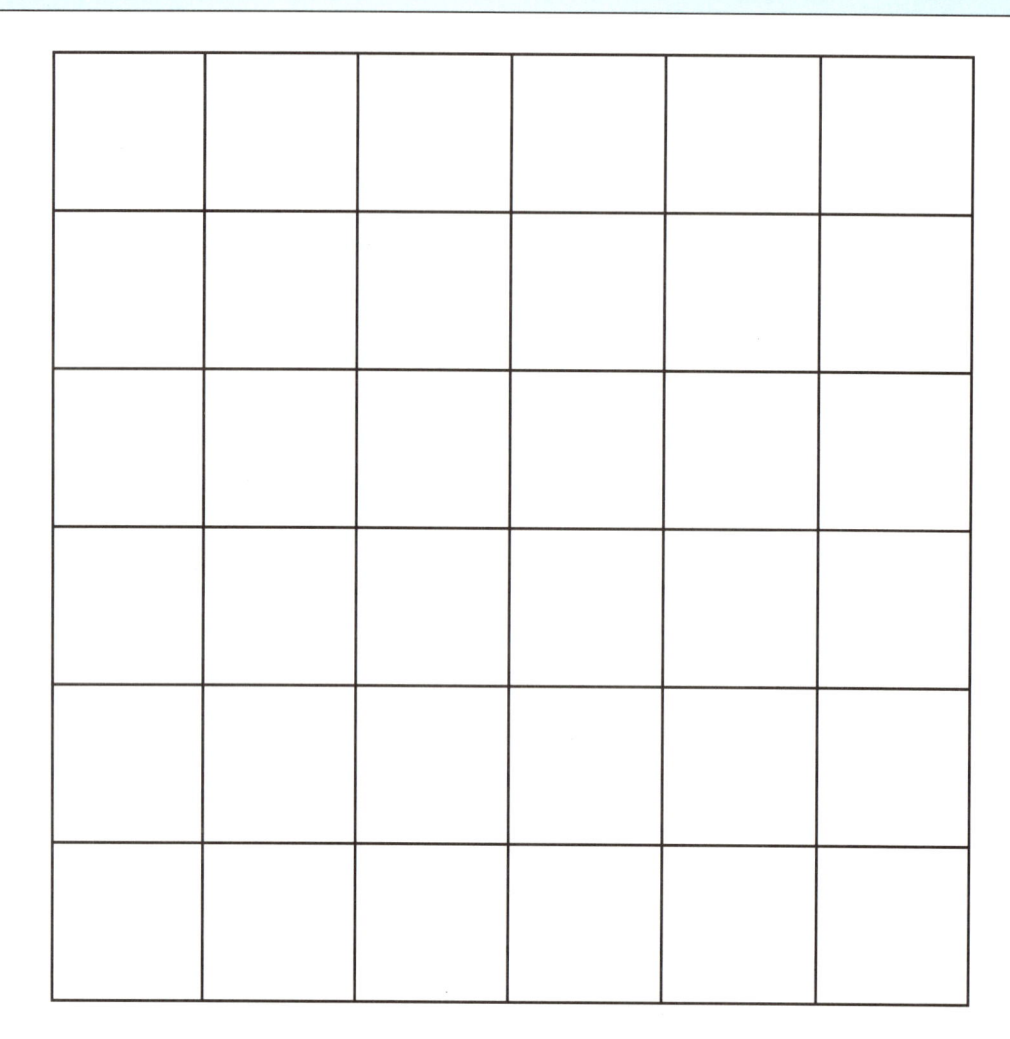

Test A

9 Rachel and Rashid were using matchsticks to make patterns with squares. Each new square is made by adding on matchsticks to the end of the pattern which comes before.

Number of squares	Number of matchsticks
1	4
2	7
3	10

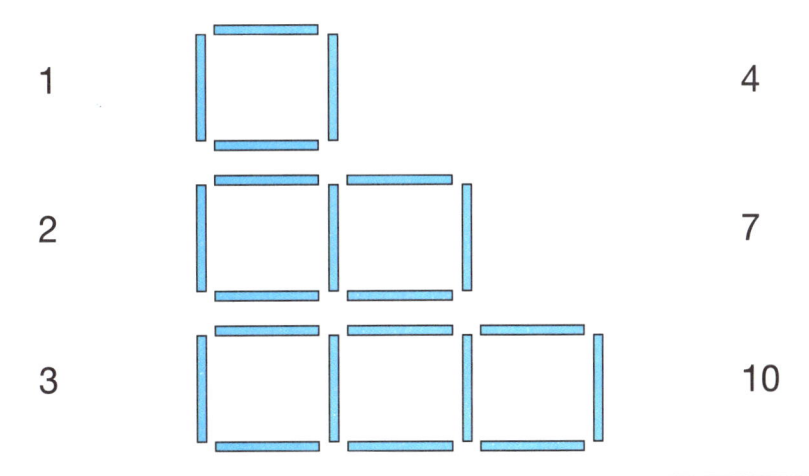

a
(i) How many matchsticks would they need to make a block of six squares?

Do not draw the squares.

.... matchsticks

(ii) Explain how you worked this out.

....

....

....

There is a rule for finding the number of matchsticks.

b Complete the number machine.

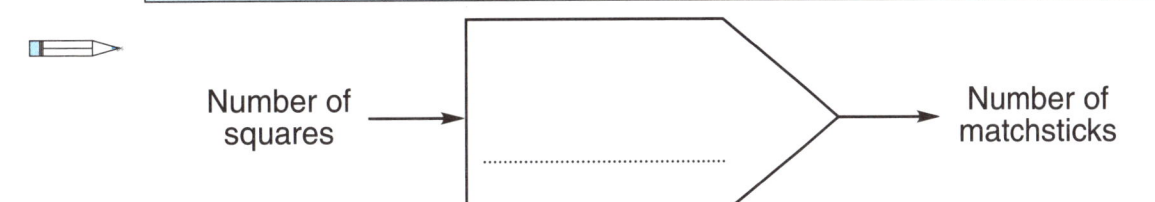

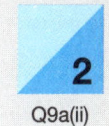

Number of squares → [....................] → Number of matchsticks

TEST A
LEVELS 3–5

MARKS

Test A

10 Five crosses are shown on this grid.

a **Draw a straight line through these five crosses.**

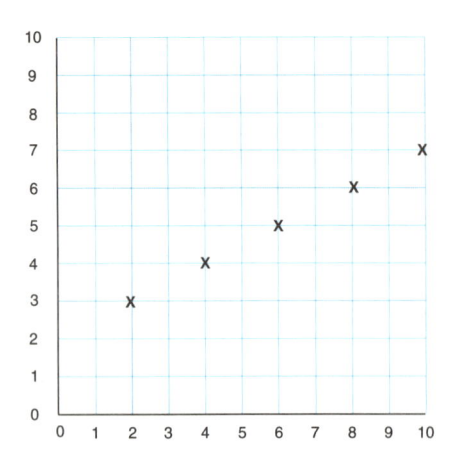

Q10a — 1

b **Write down the co-ordinates of these five crosses.**

The first two have been done for you.

(2 , 3) (4 , 4) (,) (,) (,)

Q10b — 1

c Look at the co-ordinates above. There are **TWO** patterns in these co-ordinates.

What are these two patterns?

(i) ....

(ii) ....

Q10c — 2

d The line can be extended.

Put a tick if the following co-ordinates are on this line and a cross if they are not. One has been done for you.

(0,2) ✔   (7,5.5) ☐   (9,7) ☐   (12,8) ☐

Q10d — 1

11 This question is about number patterns.

a Here is a simple number pattern.

5   10   15   20   25   30   35   40   ....

Write down the next TWO numbers in the pattern above.

Q11a — 2

12

Test A

b If you take any three numbers next to each other in the pattern and add the first and the third together and then divide by two you get the second (or middle) number. For example:

10   15   20
10 + 20 = 30
30 ÷ 2 = 15
15 is the middle number.

> **Show that this is true for the following number pattern.**

25   30   35

....

....

[2] Q11b

c Here is another number pattern.

1   1   2   3   5   8   13   21   34

In this pattern any number, after the second, is the sum of the two numbers before it. For example:
1 + 2 = 3
2 + 3 = 5

> **Write down the next TWO numbers in this pattern.**

(i) ....

[2] Q11c(i)

(ii) > **Which of the following are true about this pattern?**
> **Put a tick for true and a cross for false.**

One has been done for you.
Each number in the pattern is larger than the one before it.   ✗
Every third number in the pattern is even.   ☐
Every fourth number in the pattern has 3 as a factor.   ☐
The fourth, seventh and ninth numbers in the pattern are prime numbers.   ☐

[2] Q11c(ii)

13

12 Here are the arm reach measurements of seven children in a class:

Sam	140 cm
Laura	130 cm
Kelly	120 cm
David	115 cm
Marc	135 cm
Nathan	110 cm
Patricia	140 cm

a Finish the graph by drawing in Marc's and Laura's measurements.

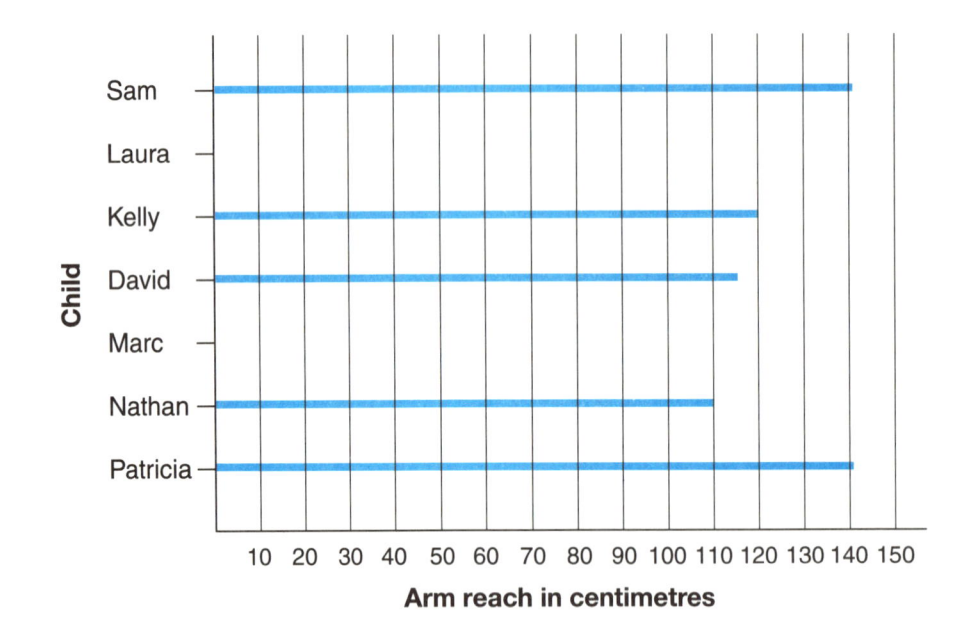

b Which **TWO** children have the *modal* arm reach?

....

c Who has the *median* reach value?

....

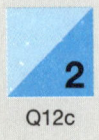

13 Pupils were putting numbers into a function machine.

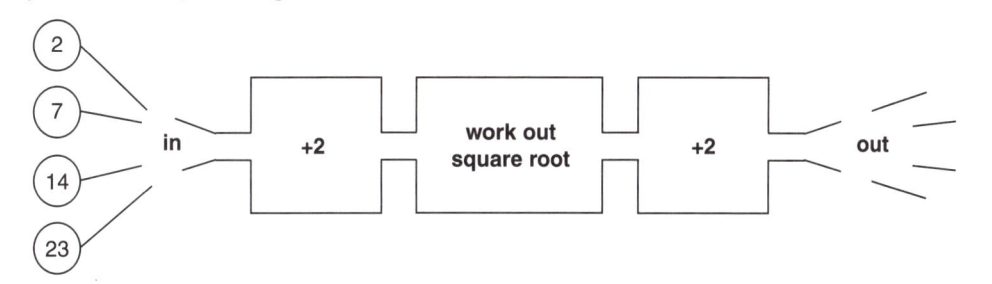

in → +2 → work out square root → +2 → out

Inputs: 2, 7, 14, 23

a Fill in the spaces.

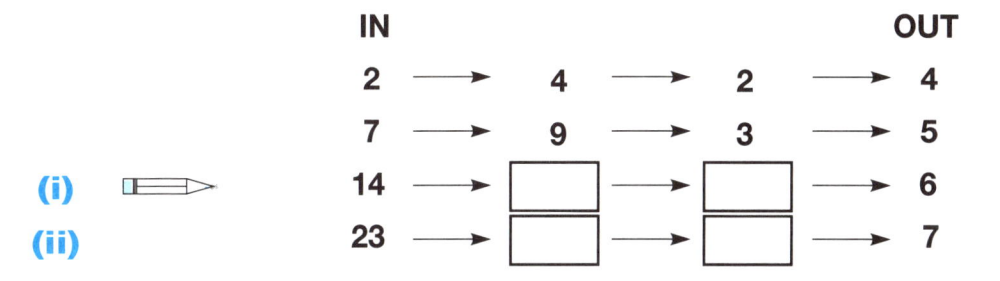

IN			OUT
2 →	4 →	2 →	4
7 →	9 →	3 →	5
(i) 14 →	☐ →	☐ →	6
(ii) 23 →	☐ →	☐ →	7

There is a pattern in the numbers being put into the machine and in the numbers coming out.

b If 8 comes out of the machine, what number goes in?

Test B

TEST B LEVELS 3–5

MARKS

CALCULATOR CAN BE USED

Start ☐   Finish ☐

1 There are four families living in Weston Road. They are:

Mr and Mrs Singh at number one hundred and seventy-three

Mr and Mrs Jones at number ninety-five

Mr and Mrs Hussein at number two hundred and forty-one

Mr and Mrs Smith at number one hundred and forty-eight.

The postman delivers letters to the houses in order, starting with the lowest number and finishing with the highest.

a To which of these four houses does the postman go first?

....

b To which of these four houses does the postman go last?

....

c Whose house number divides exactly by two?

....

Miss Evans lives at number one hundred and seven.

d Finish the address on the envelope.

> Miss D. Evans
>   Weston Road
> Hambleton
> Suffolk
> IP7 4HN

Q1a — 1
Q1b — 1
Q1c — 1
Q1d — 1

16

Test B

2

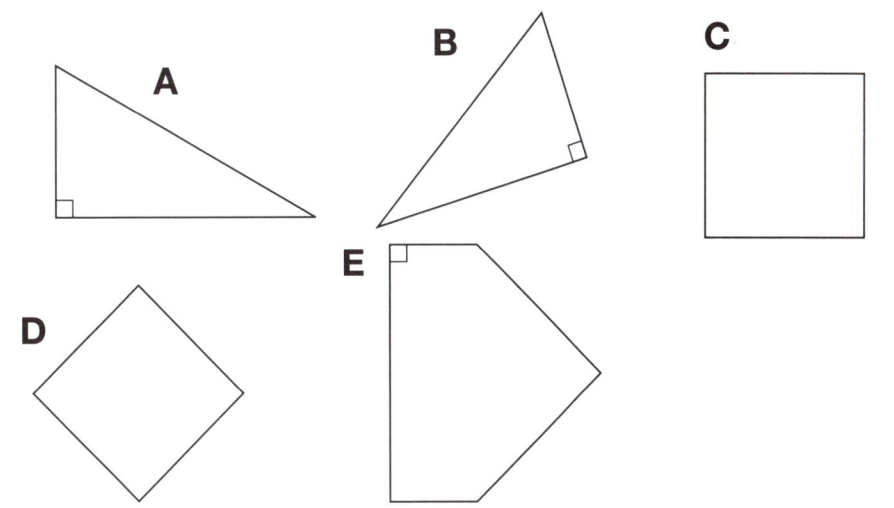

Shapes **A** and **B** are triangles.
Shapes **C** and **D** are squares.
Shape **E** is a pentagon.

a Write down **TWO** things which are the same about all of the shapes.

....

....

b Which shapes are quadrilaterals?

Shape ☐ and shape ☐

c Draw a hexagon which contains **ONE** right angle on the grid below.

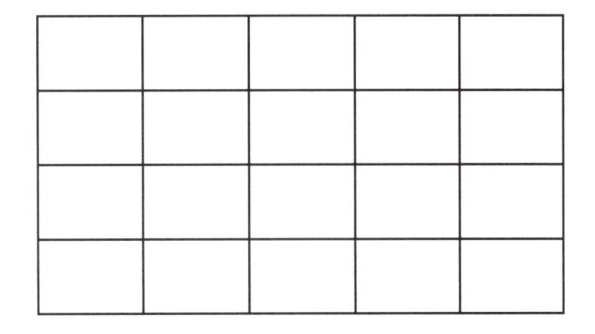

TEST B
LEVELS 3–5

MARKS

2
Q2a

1
Q2b

1
Q2c

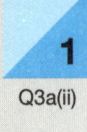

3a A first class stamp costs 26p.

Omar has £2 in his pocket.

(i) **How many first class stamps can he buy for £2?**

....

(ii) **How much money will he still have?**

....

b **Finish this shopping list.**

Potatoes   4kg at £0.49 a kg   £1.96

(i) Bananas   2kg at £1.10 a kg

(ii) Apples   1.5kg at £1.90 a kg

4 Here are some shapes. There is a square, two isosceles triangles, one equilateral triangle and a rhombus.

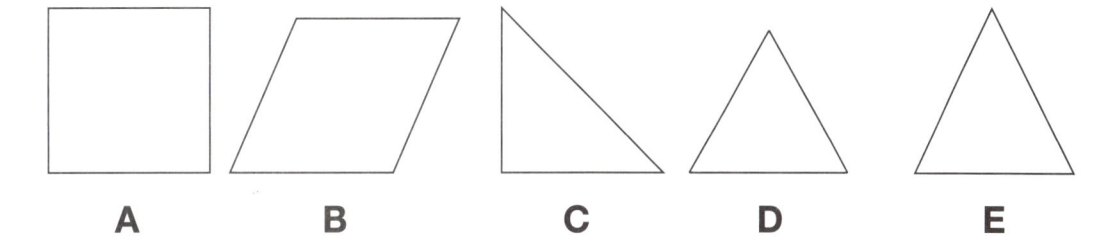

A   B   C   D   E

a Finish the table. One has been done for you.

Shape	Number of sides	Number of sides of equal length	Number of right angles
A	4	4	4
B			
C			
D			
E			

b A rhombus has four sides of equal length and no angle is a right angle.

Which of the shapes above is a rhombus?

....

c

Shape	Number of sides	Number of sides of equal length	Number of right angles
F	4	2	2

Draw a shape which could be F.

19

5 Three golfers compare their results over six rounds of golf.

Golfer	1st	2nd	3rd	4th	5th	6th	Mean or average	Range
Alice	100	87	85	98	112	94	96.0	27
Betty	94	99	97	99	90	99	96.3	9
Chris	102	104	104	103	102	103	103.0	2

In golf, low scores are better than high scores.

Betty was picked to represent the golf club in a competition rather than Alice or Chris.

Explain why Betty was chosen rather than Chris or Alice. You must use the words *mean* and *range* in your answers.

a Betty was chosen instead of Chris because: ....

....

b Betty was chosen instead of Alice because: ....

....

6 Here is a pattern of squares.

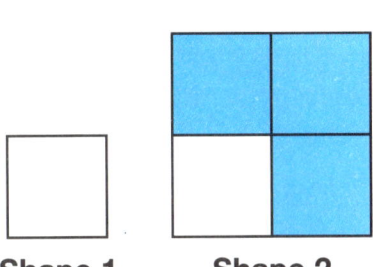

Shape 1   Shape 2   Shape 3

The total number of blue and white small squares in each shape makes a number pattern.

a **Draw and shade the next shape in the pattern, Shape 4.**

b **Continue this pattern by filling in all the missing numbers.**

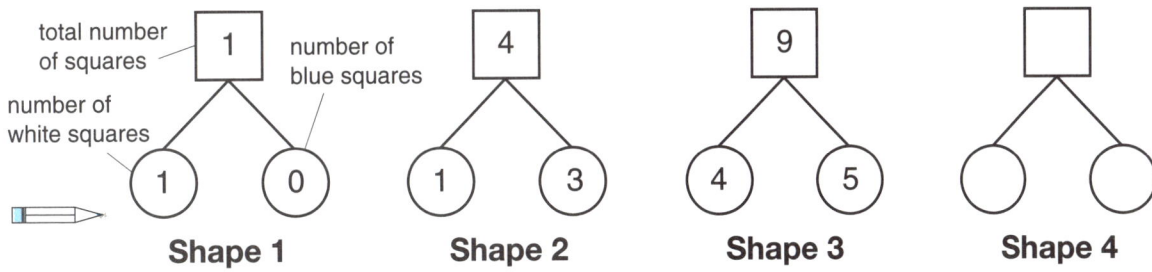

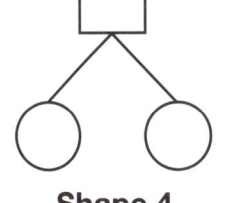

total number of squares — 1   number of blue squares   4   9   ☐

number of white squares

① ⓪   ① ③   ④ ⑤   ○ ○

Shape 1   Shape 2   Shape 3   Shape 4

c **Write down ONE thing that you notice about the numbers in the circles.**

7 At the school Summer Fayre there are lots of things to do. Each go on the Bouncy Castle costs £1.35.

a Write the cost of **FIVE** goes on the Bouncy Castle.

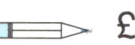

£ ....

b On the spinning arrow game there is a prize if the arrow lands on number 1.

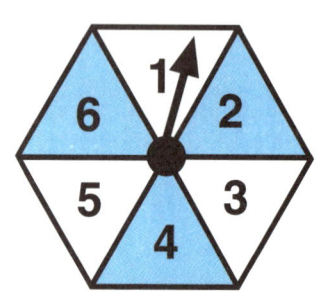

Here is a probability line.

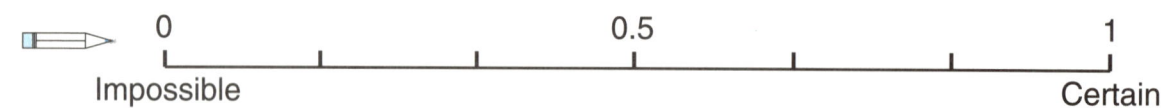

0 — Impossible ———— 0.5 ———— 1 — Certain

(i) Place a cross on the line above to show the probability of the arrow landing on number 1.

(ii) Explain why you have put the cross in that place.

....

....

Here is another probability line.

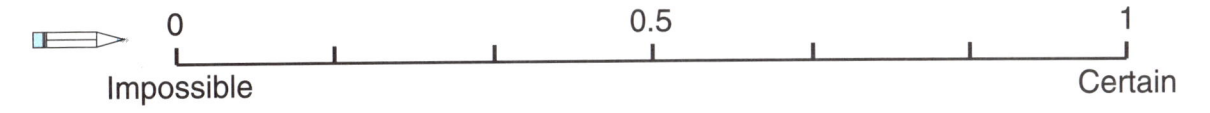

```
0                    0.5                    1
|----|----|----|----|----|----|----|----|----|----|
Impossible                              Certain
```

(iii) Put a cross on the line to show the probability of the arrow landing on an even number.

(iv) Explain why you have put the cross in that place.

....

....

c   Forty per cent of the money made at the Summer Fayre was given to the local old people's centre and 60% to the school fund.

The Summer Fayre made £900.

How much was given to the old people's centre? Show your working.

8 The price of petrol at a petrol station is often shown in two ways: price per litre and price per gallon.

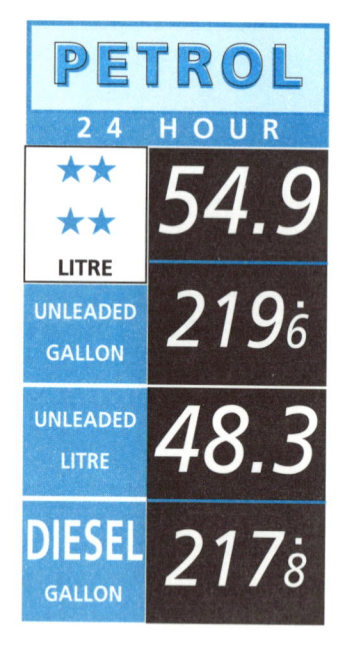

PETROL
24 HOUR

★★ ★★ LITRE	54.9
UNLEADED GALLON	219.6
UNLEADED LITRE	48.3
DIESEL GALLON	217.8

The graph is a conversion graph to enable you to change from one to the other.

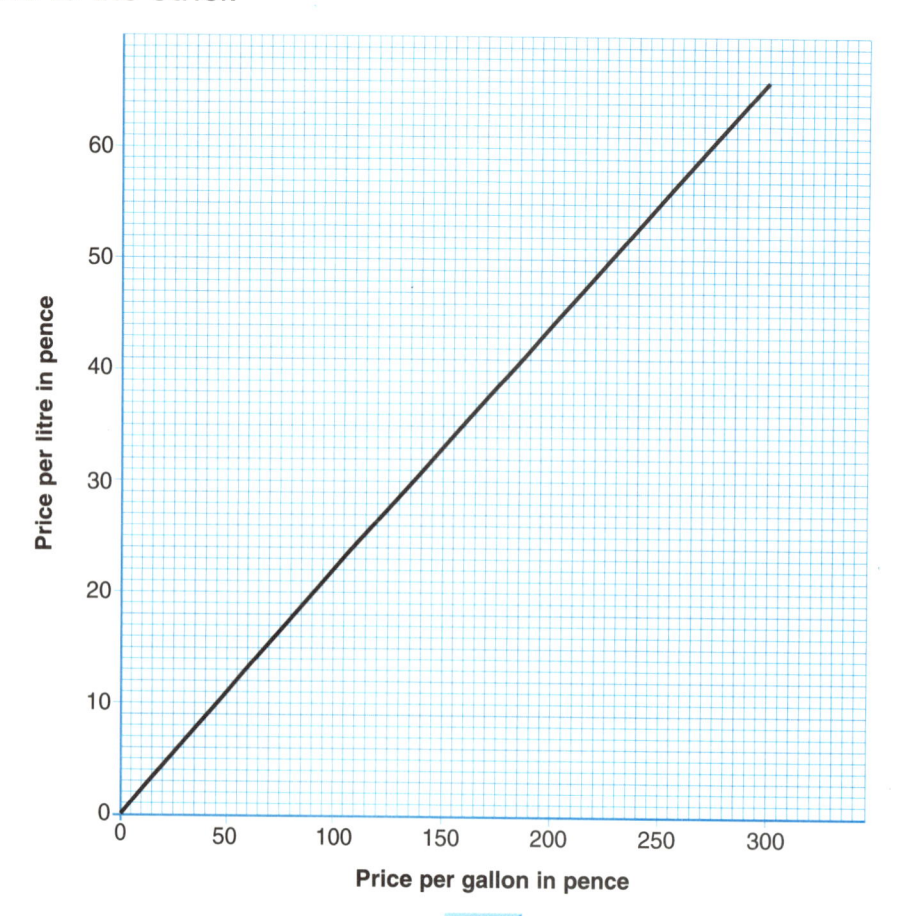

Test B

a **What is the price of a gallon of petrol which costs 55p per litre?**

✏️ ....

b The petrol then rises from 55p by 2p per litre.

What is the *rise* in the cost of a gallon of petrol?

✏️ ....

c Use the information on the advertising sign at the start of this question.

Work out the number of litres in a gallon.

✏️ .... litres

9

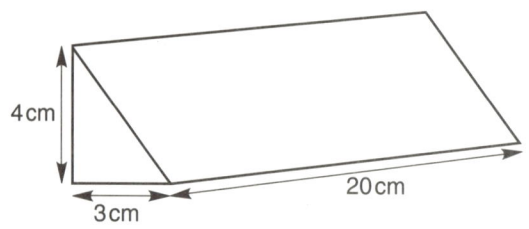

The drawing shows a cardboard gift box.

This gift box can be made from the net shown below. The flaps are not shown.

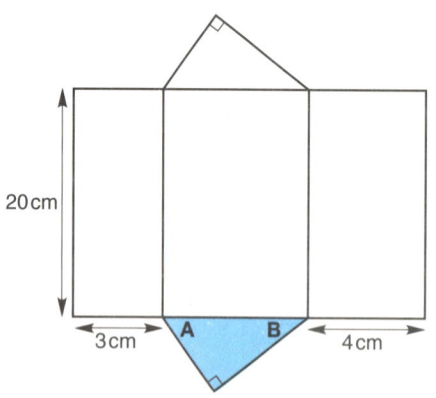

Area of a triangle = ½ × base × height.

a Finish the accurate drawing of the shaded triangle.

A ——————————— B

b What is the area of the shaded triangle?

.... cm²

c Use a protractor or angle measurer to measure the size of angle A on your triangle.

....

10 These shapes are all made with triangles.
The sides of each triangle are 1 cm long.

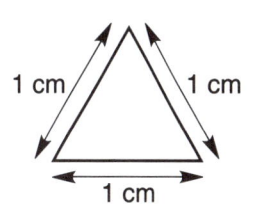

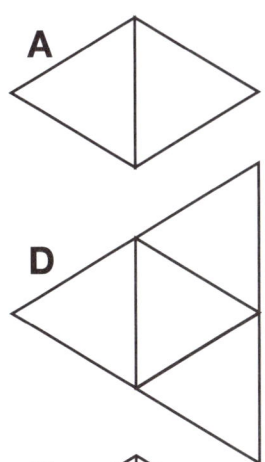

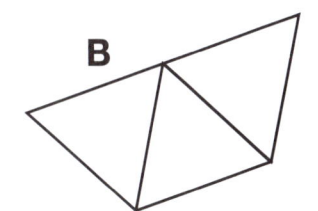

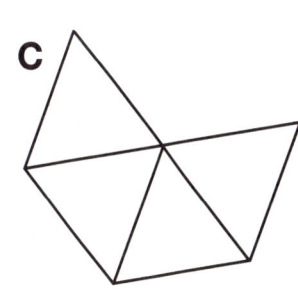

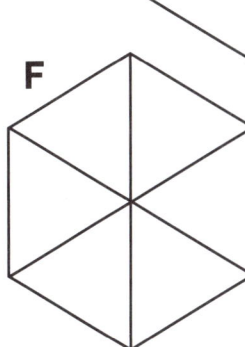

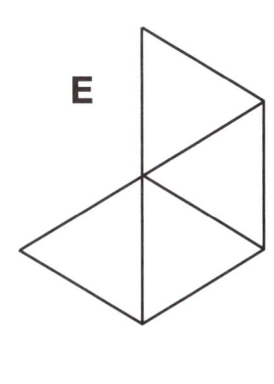

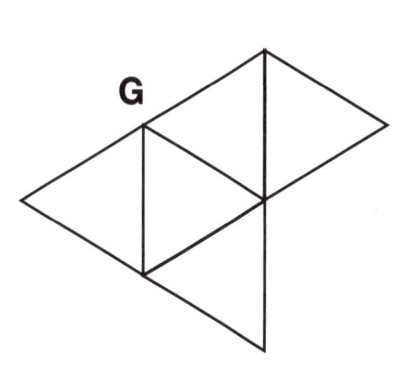

a Which shape will fold to make a pyramid with a solid base?

b Which shape has the largest area?

c Which shape has the longest perimeter?

d Which two shapes are congruent?

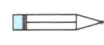

11 Andrew enters the digits 1, 4 and 5 into his calculator in different ways. He uses all 3 digits each time.

The first number that he makes is | 4 | 5 | 1 |

a **Write down two even numbers that he can make.**

✏️ ▭▭▭ and ▭▭▭

b **What two numbers can he make which have 5 as a factor?**

✏️ ▭▭▭ and ▭▭▭

c Andrew then uses a new number key | ? | to enter some four digit numbers.

Which number key has he used if

| 4 | 5 | 1 | ? | is a multiple of 18

✏️ | ? | = ▭

d Can you make a 3 digit number which is both a SQUARE number and a MULTIPLE of 12?
(You can use any digit but each one must be different)

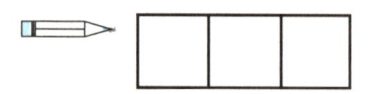

✏️ ▭▭▭

Test B

12 Gemma and Simon make a game where they each score points on throwing a die. If the score is even, Gemma scores the points shown on the die. If the score is odd, Simon scores in the same way.

The two children play for 5 minutes and then total their points to see who has won.

Here are the scores on the die:

4 6 1 2 1 1 6 2 1 1 6 4 4 3
3 2 5 1 5 5 1 3 6 2 2 3 1 3

a Complete the following frequency tables.

GEMMA

Score	Count
2	
4	
6	

SIMON

Score	Count
1	
3	
5	

b Simon scored a total of 38 points.

What did Gemma score?

c

(i) Do you think that the game was fair?

(ii) Give a reason for your answer.

TEST C
LEVEL 6

MARKS

CALCULATOR CAN BE USED

Test C

Start ☐ Finish ☐

1 A computer program displays the same number in three ways.

Window 1 shows the number as a decimal.
Window 2 shows the number as a fraction in its lowest form.
Window 3 shows a percentage.

Complete the missing windows.

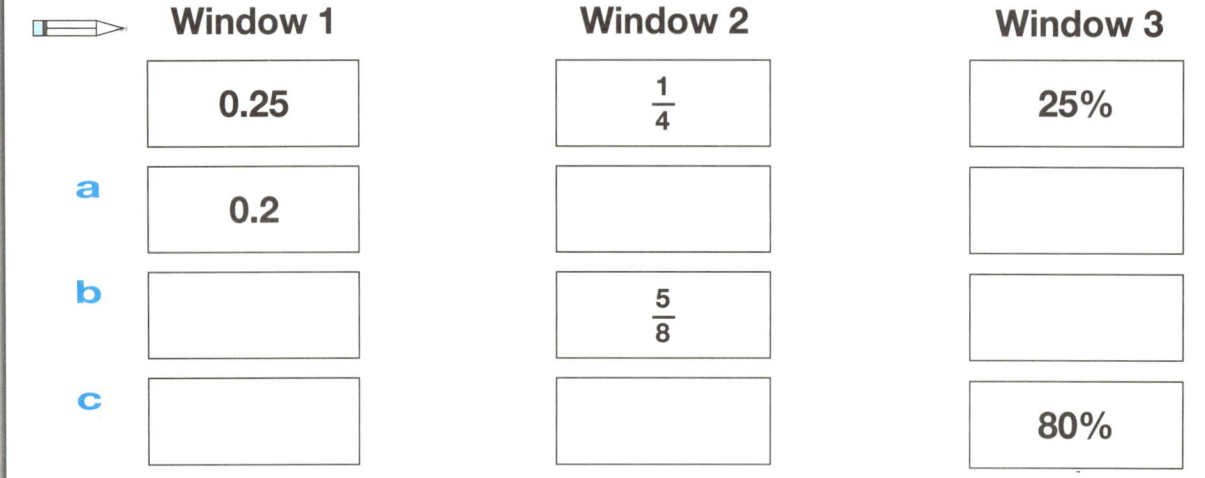

Window 1	Window 2	Window 3
0.25	$\frac{1}{4}$	25%

a | 0.2 | | |

b | | $\frac{5}{8}$ | |

c | | | 80% |

3 Q1

2 A pair of scales is used to balance two kinds of boxes, **A** boxes and **B** boxes.

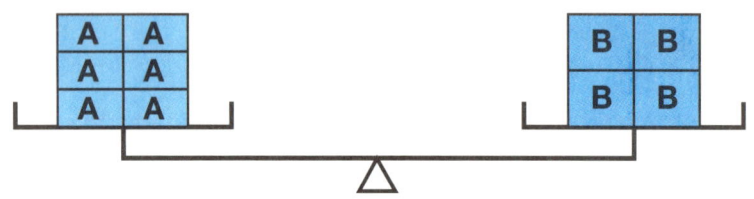

a One **A** box weighs 2 kg.

How much does one B box weigh?

1 Q2a

.... kg

A second pair of scales is balanced using seven **C** boxes and weights as shown:

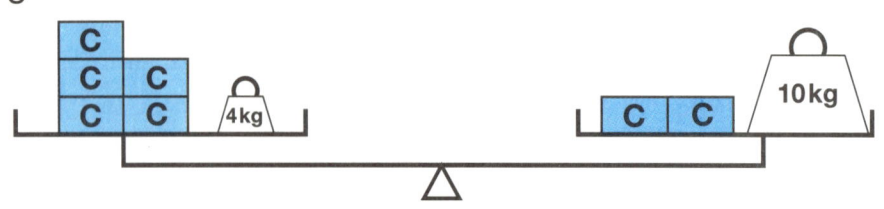

30

Test C

b Complete the equation which shows the balancing scales.

5C + ☐ = ☐ + 10

c Find the weight of one **C** box.

.... kg

3 The vertices of a shape have the co-ordinates:
(−3, 1) (−4, 4) (−2, 4) (−1, 1)

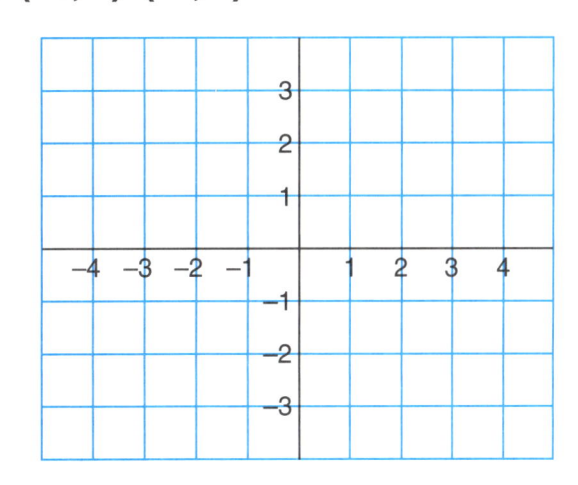

a Draw the shape on the grid.

b Draw a second shape which is a reflection of the first in the line $x = 0$.

c Write down the co-ordinates of the second shape.

....

d What kind of shape have you drawn?

....

31

4 Kate and Frances play a game using a die numbered 1 to 6 and a spinner marked as shown:

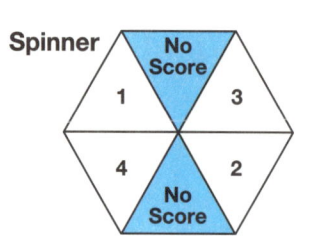

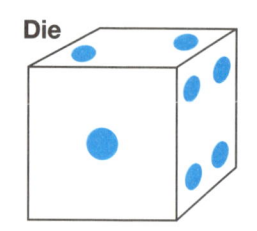

Spinner: 1, No Score, 3, 2, No Score, 4

To decide who goes first, the score on the die is added to the score on the spinner.

a What is the highest possible score?

....

During the early part of the game, the spinner is used on its own.

b What is the chance of a 'No Score'?

....

Later in the game, the score on the die is again added to the score on the spinner.

The girls cannot agree which scores occur most often so they decide to draw up a table of possible totals.

c Complete the table.

Die score

	1	2	3	4	5	6
		2				
				4		
						10

Spinner score

32

d Which possible totals occur most often?

....

e What is the probability of scoring a total of 2?

....

5 Year 6 are visiting the local museum.

25% of the children see the Victorian toys collection.
12.5% of the children buy souvenirs from the shop.
24 children take photographs.

Eight children see the Victorian toys collection.

a How many children visit the museum?

.... children

b How many children buy souvenirs?

.... children

c What percentage of the Year 6 children take photographs?

....

6 In Technology, Laura and Alec are testing wind-up model cars. They find that the number of times each wheel turns is directly connected to the number of 'winds'.

5 winds produce 15 turns of each wheel.

a **How many wheel turns will 7 winds produce?**

.... wheel turns

b **How many winds are needed for 9 wheel turns?**

.... winds

A car travels 30 cm with 6 turns of every wheel.

c **How far will it travel with 4 winds?**

.... cm

7 A carton manufacturer makes a box which has a net as shown below (the flaps are not shown).

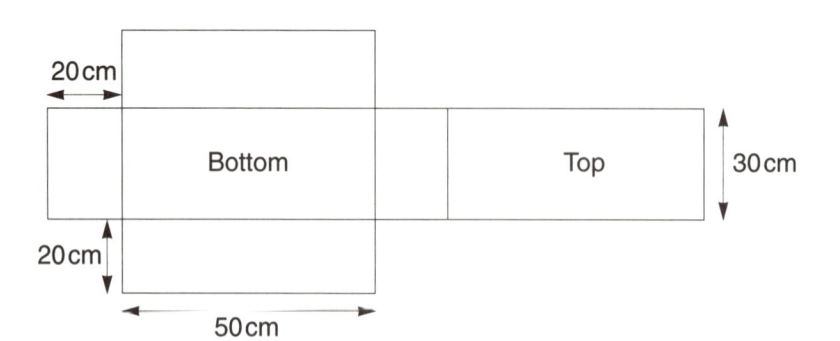

20 cm ← → Bottom | Top | 30 cm
20 cm
50 cm

a **How much card is used to make one box?**

.... cm²

Test C

The top of the box has a disc of card removed so that crisp bags can be taken out easily.

The disc has a diameter of 20 cm.

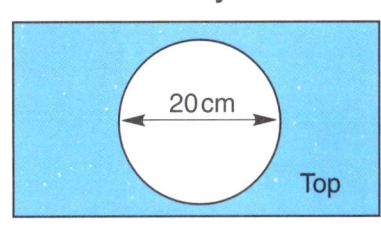

20 cm
Top

Area of a circle = πr^2
Use $\pi = 3.14$

b **What is the area of the disc which is removed?**

.... cm²

8 This pattern shows blue squares surrounding white squares.

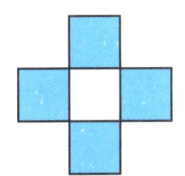

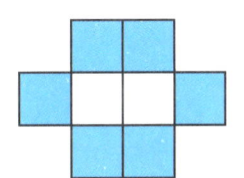

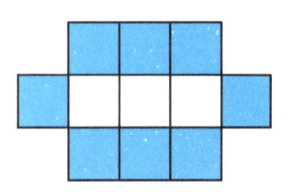

a **Complete the mapping.**

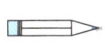

White	Blue
1 →	4
2 →	
3 →	
4 →	
5 →	

b **Without drawing, work out how many blue squares will surround 20 white squares.**

c **Describe briefly how to work out the number of blue squares if you are given the number of white ones.**

9 Jane is hanging weights on the end of a spring.

She then measures the height, in centimetres, of the end of the spring from the floor with different weights on the spring.

Below is a graph of her results.

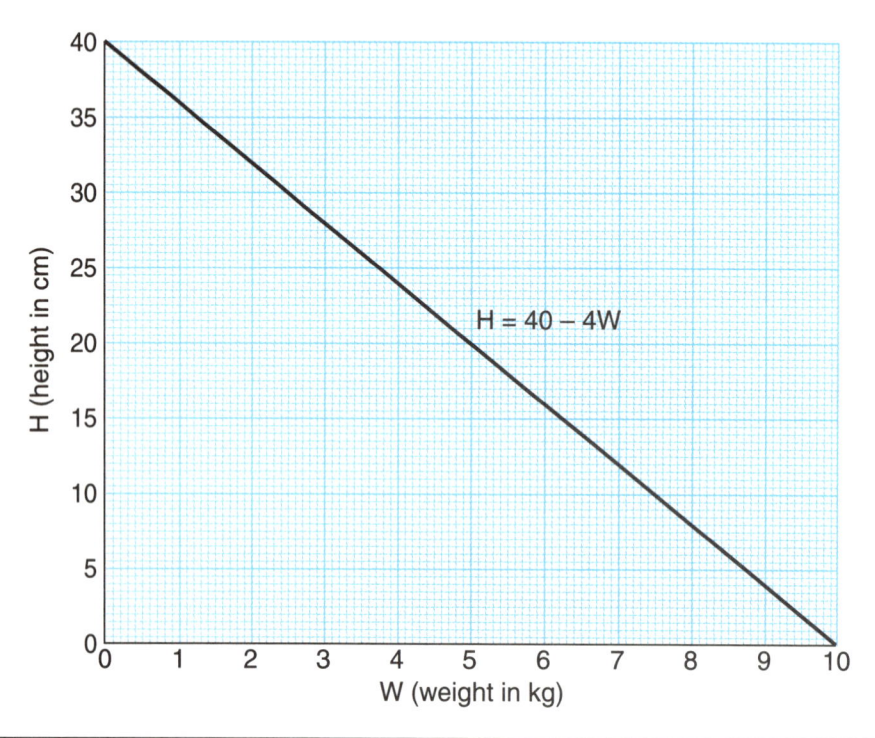

$H = 40 - 4W$

a From the graph, what height off the floor will the spring be with a weight of 8 kg attached?

.... cm

b What weight will hold the spring 15 cm off the floor?

.... kg

c What is the smallest weight that will make the spring touch the floor?

.... kg

Mental Arithmetic

Ask your parents to detach page 55 and read out the questions for this test to you. You should write the answers on the lines below.

1 ....

2 ....

3 ....

4 ....

5 ....

6 ....

7 ....

8 ....

9 ....

10 ....

11 ....

12 ....

13 ....

14 ....

15 ....

16 ....

17 ....

18 ....

19 ....

20 ....

Answers

HOW TO MARK THE QUESTIONS
When marking your child's test remember that the answers given are sample answers. You must look at your child's answers and judge whether they deserve credit. Award the mark if the answer deserves credit.

There is no automatic penalty for a word that is misspelt. Look at the word as written and read it aloud. If it sounds correct and has the correct number of syllables, the mark can be awarded.

When you go through the test with your child try to be positive. Look for good things that have been done in addition to showing where errors have been made.

Enter your child's marks for each test on the Marking Grid on page 58, and then work out your child's level of achievement on these tests on page 57.

TEST A **Pages 2–15**

1 a	124	1 mark
b (i)	412	1 mark
(ii)	421	1 mark
		Total 3 marks

Note to parent
This is an easy introduction to the magnitude of numbers which can be made from three number cards.

2 a	E and H	Both required: 1 mark
b	One mirror line drawn on each shape	2 marks
		Total 3 marks

E   H   or   H

Note to parent
This question is about the reflective symmetry of capital letters. If you put a mirror vertically along the mirror line, the image in the mirror will complete the shape of the letter exactly.

It is worthwhile trying other letters for reflective symmetry.

Test A Answers

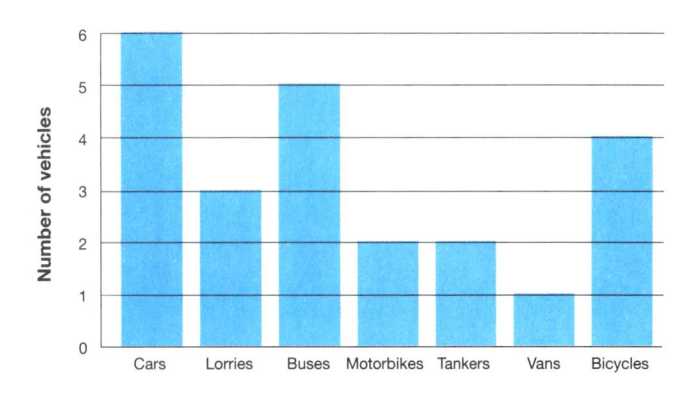

3 a 20 — *1 mark*
b 9 — *1 mark*
c

[Bar chart: Cars 6, Lorries 3, Buses 5, Motorbikes 2, Tankers 2, Vans 1, Bicycles 4; y-axis: Number of vehicles]

1 mark

d Thursday — 3 cars

Friday — 3½ cars

N.B. Half a car represents 1 vehicle.

One for each day: 2 marks
Total 5 marks

Note to parent
This is a data handling question. Children use these skills in all curriculum areas.

4 a 7 boxes — *2 marks*
   working out: 40 ÷ 6 (or similar)
b 4 — *1 mark*
Total 3 marks

Note to parent
Many children divide 40 by 6 and give the answer 6. They forget the other 4 eggs must be placed in a box.

5 a 12744 — *1 mark*
   working out: 12960 − 216 (or similar)
b 25920 — *1 mark*
   working out: 12960 × 2 (or similar)
c 60 — *1 mark*
d 30 — *1 mark*
Total 4 marks

Note to parent
For **a** and **b**, there is no mark awarded for answers worked out by a simple long multiplication method. This question tests children's understanding of number operations and how, given one number fact, it is possible to work out related answers. Help for this question can be given in the form of number patterns, for example:

4 × 3 = 12; 4 × 30 = 120; 40 × 30 = 1200; 40 × 15 = 600   etc.

Test A Answers

6 a 100 people — *1 mark*
  b Coronation Street — *1 mark*
  c Brookside — *1 mark*
  d EastEnders — *1 mark*
  e The survey could be more reliable if a larger number of people were questioned, or the same people were questioned each time. — *1 mark*
  Total 5 marks

> **Note to parent**
>
> The results of a simple survey are this time displayed in pie charts. In question 3 results were displayed on a bar chart. It is possible to buy a template in a good stationer to enable pie charts to be drawn more easily.

7 a 5 — *1 mark*
  b 1 — *1 mark*
  c 4 — *1 mark*
  d 9 — *1 mark*
  Total 4 marks

> **Note to parent**
>
> Looking at car wheels provides opportunities for testing rotational symmetry. In order to do this, your child should trace the shape of the wheel and then rotate it through one revolution. How many times in one revolution is the shape the same?

8 A suitable shape would be:

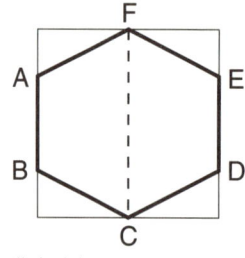

Six-sided shape
AB and DE parallel
Mirror line - - - - -

Award one mark if parallel sides.
Award one mark if six sides.
Award one mark if reflective symmetry. — *3 marks*
Total 3 marks

> **Note to parent**
>
> There is more than one possible answer so you have to look at the answer given and see if it fits.

9 a (i) 19 — *1 mark*
   (ii) Adding one square adds 3 matchsticks — *1 mark*
       Three squares added, so 9 extra matchsticks — *1 mark*
   b × 3 + 1 — *1 mark*
  Total 4 marks

Test A Answers

Note to parent

Again, this question is about patterns and links with simple algebra. You could try further examples and look for different patterns. For example:

◇ 4   ◇◇ 8   ◇◇◇ 12

The number of matchsticks is equal to four times the number of squares, m = 4n.

---

10 a Straight line through the five crosses — *1 mark*
b (6,5) (8,6) (10,7) — *All three: 1 mark*
c (i) The first number increases by two each time. — *1 mark*
(ii) The second number increases by one each time. — *1 mark*
d Ticks in (7,5.5) and (12,8) and not in (9,7) — *All three: 1 mark*

Total 5 marks

Note to parent

Co-ordinates are frequently used in mathematics papers. In this question only positive values of *x* and *y* are used. It is possible to use co-ordinates in the four quadrants.

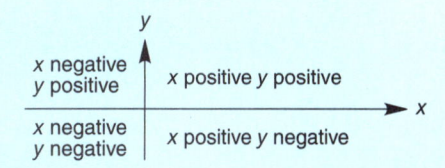

x negative, y positive	x positive y positive
x negative, y negative	x positive y negative

It is important that the horizontal axis is the *x*-axis and the vertical axis is the *y*-axis. When writing the co-ordinates of a point the value on the *x*-axis is first and the value on the *y*-axis is second. So a value of $x = 4$ and $y = 5$ is recorded as (4,5). In other words, when recording the co-ordinates of a point you go across and then up. You may appreciate that all of the points in the question are on a straight line:
$y = \frac{1}{2}x + 2$
Your child is not expected to know this at KS2.

---

11 a 45   50 — *2 marks*
b 25 + 35 = 60 — *1 mark*
  60 ÷ 2 = 30 — *1 mark*
c (i) 55, 89 — *2 marks*
(ii) Ticks for second and third statements — *1 mark*
  but not for last statement — *1 mark*

Total 8 marks

Note to parent

In part **a** the sequence of numbers is easy to see. The numbers increase by 5 each time or are the sequence of numbers in the 5 times table. Part **b** is the Fibonacci series, named after the thirteenth century Italian mathematician who devised it. Each term in the series is the sum of the previous two terms.

Test A Answers

12 a

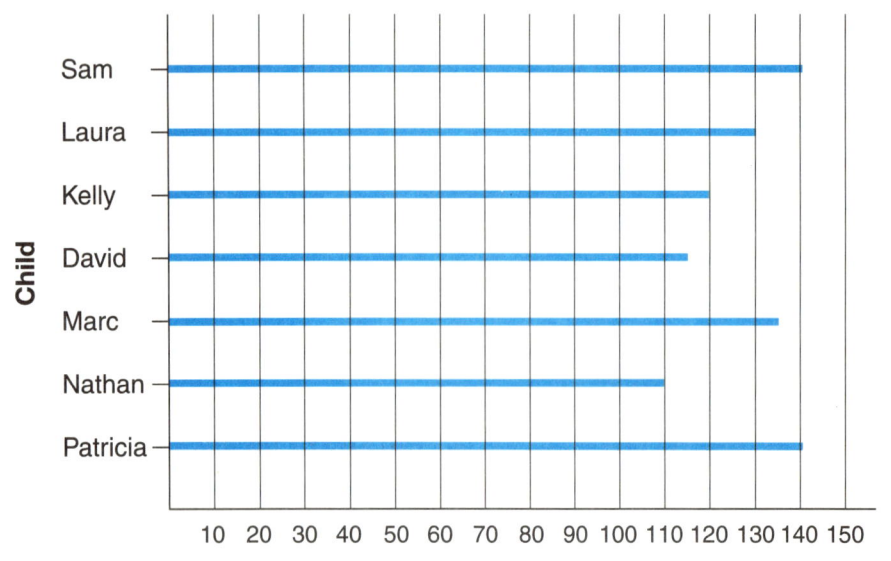

Bar chart: Arm reach in centimetres (x-axis) vs Child (y-axis)
- Sam: 140
- Laura: 130
- Kelly: 120
- David: 115
- Marc: 135
- Nathan: 110
- Patricia: 140

1 mark

b Sam and Patricia   *1 mark*
c Laura   *2 marks*
   Working out: arrange the measures in ascending order.
   110 115 120 130 135 140 140
   Laura has the middle value.

Total 4 marks

Note to parent

Measures of average form part of Attainment Target 4: 'Handling Data'. The *mode* is the most frequent occurrence of a value from a group of values. The *median* is the middle value – measurements must first be arranged in ascending order of size.

13 a (i) 16 4
   (ii) 25 5   *2 marks*
   b 34   *2 marks*

Total 4 marks

Note to parent

This question is about number machines and also requires the understanding of square roots and inverses.

TEST TOTAL 55 MARKS

Test B Answers

TEST B *Pages 16–29*

1 a 95 *or* Mr and Mrs Jones' house — *1 mark*
b 241 *or* Mr and Mrs Hussein's house — *1 mark*
c Mr and Mrs Smith's house — *1 mark*
d 107, Weston Rd — *1 mark*
Total 4 marks

Note to parent

This question is about sequencing numbers and numbers which divide by 2 and 5. Appreciating the place values of numbers is important; for example, appreciating the difference between 107 and 170. If your child has difficulty with these questions, make some cards with numbers up to 999 and get him or her to arrange them in ascending order.

2 a All shapes shown contain one or more right angles. All have straight line sides. — *2 marks*
b Shapes **C** and **D** — *1 mark*
c Any six-sided shape with one right angle is acceptable. — *1 mark*
Total 4 marks

Note to parent

This question is about identifying and classifying shapes. A mirror can be used to help identify those shapes with line symmetry.

3 a (i) 7 — *1 mark*
(ii) 18p — *1 mark*
b (i) £2.20 — *1 mark*
(ii) £2.85 — *1 mark*
Total 4 marks

Note to parent

Your child should appreciate that £2 will buy 7 stamps but will not buy 8. First your child should realise that £2 is 200 pence, then divide 200p by 26. He or she must ignore any decimal numbers and give an answer of 7. It is easy to find other examples your child can try.

Test B Answers

4 a

Shape	Number of sides	Number of sides of equal length	Number of right angles
B	4	4	0
C	3	2	1
D	3	3	0
E	3	2	0

Award 2 marks if nine or more correct.
Award 1 mark if five to eight correct.
Award 0 marks if four or less correct.   **2 marks**

b B   *1 mark*

c *This is one possible answer:*

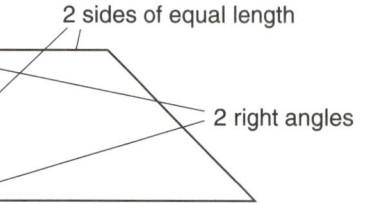

2 sides of equal length

2 right angles   *1 mark*

Total 4 marks

Note to parent

The answer given in **c** is just one example – others could be drawn. Look at the shape your child has drawn. Award only one mark if:
- the shape has four sides
- no two sides are of the same length
- there are two right angles.

5 a Betty has a lower mean than Chris.   *1 mark*
It is more likely that she will score a lower score.   *1 mark*
b Betty and Alice have almost identical means.   *1 mark*
Betty has a much smaller range and so is more consistent.   *1 mark*

Total 4 marks

Note to parent

Here, data has been given about the scores of three golfers. The question is at Level 5 and requires the appreciation of how to use the mean (or average) and the range. Your child will also need to know the meaning of the terms *mode* and *median*. Look at this series of numbers:

3 3 2 4 5 3 4

The mean is what we commonly call the 'average'. Add the numbers up and divide by 7: the mean is approximately 3.4. The range is the difference between the lowest and highest, i.e. 3. The mode is the most common number, i.e. 3. Now arrange the numbers in ascending order: **2 3 3 3 4 4 5**. The median is the middle one, i.e. 3.

Test B Answers

6a

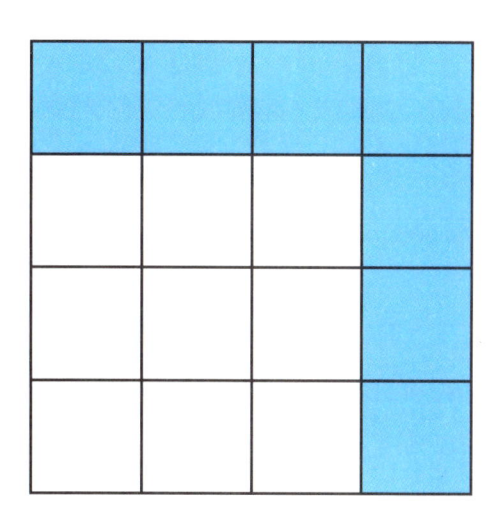

1 mark

b

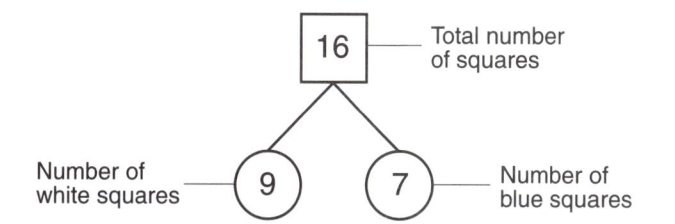

16 — Total number of squares

Number of white squares — 9   7 — Number of blue squares

2 marks

(*All three numbers are required for the 2 marks.*)

c *Suitable answers would include one of the following:*
The odd number pattern 3, 5, 7
The square number pattern 1, 4, 9

Note to parent

This question is about establishing patterns. If your child has got this question right, ask him or her to work out the next two sets of numbers in the pattern.

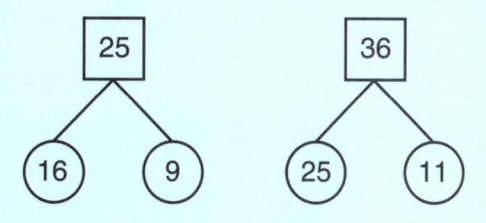

25 — 16, 9
36 — 25, 11

Your child could then check his or her answers by drawing out the squares and counting up. Again, 1 cm squared paper is useful.

Test B Answers

7 a £6.75 — *1 mark*
 b (i)

```
0           0.5              1
|____X___|____|____|____|____|
Impossible                Certain
```
1 mark

(ii) There are six possible answers but only one will be number 1. — *1 mark*

(iii)
```
0           0.5              1
|____|____|____X____|____|____|
Impossible                Certain
```
1 mark

(iv) There are six possible answers but only three are even (2, 4 and 6). — *1 mark*

 c $\frac{40}{100} \times 900 = £360$ for the old people's centre — *2 marks*

Total 7 marks

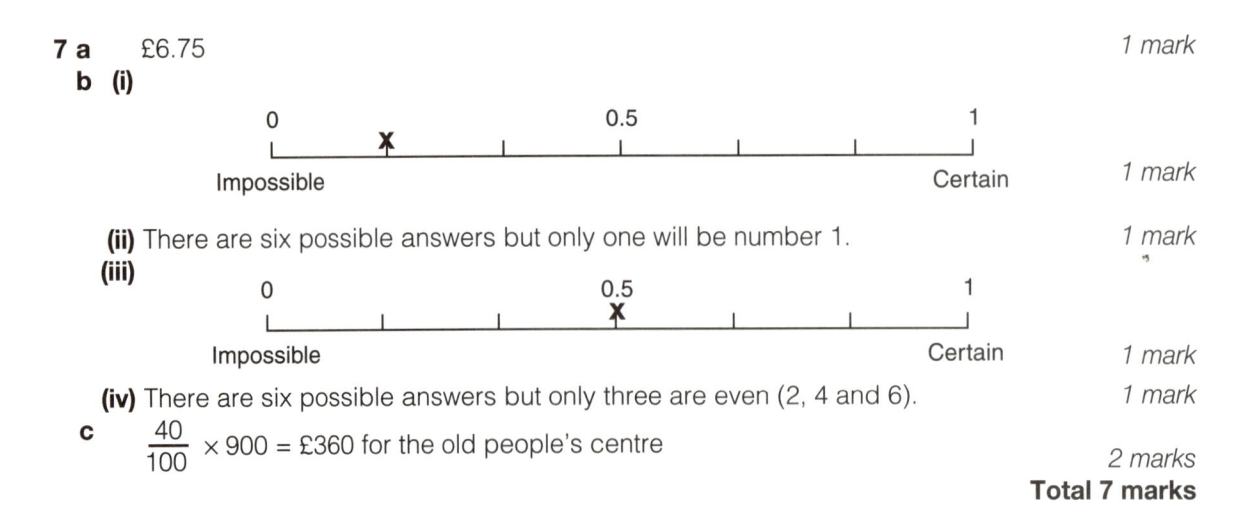

Note to parent

This question provides practice in the use of a calculator and examples of questions on probability. Sometimes we, who learnt mathematics without the aid of a calculator, feel that children should be able to do everything without a calculator. The routine arithmetical aspects of this question are best done with a calculator. The child still has to appreciate the mathematical processes involved.

8 a £2.50 per gallon (This should be obtained from the graph.) — *1 mark*
 b 10p approximately — *1 mark*
 c 219.6 ÷ 48.3 (Divide price per gallon by price per litre.) — *2 marks*
 = 4.547

Total 4 marks

Note to parent

Here we are looking at a conversion graph. Often conversion graphs are shown in other contexts. It is possible to use other prices and practise further. In part **c** your child has to realise that unleaded petrol costs the same whether it is sold in litres or gallons. It is important to use the right information from the display sign, i.e. unleaded in both cases.

Test B Answers

9 a Look at your child's drawing.
The two sides should measure 3 cm and 4 cm.
The angle opposite the longest side should be a right angle. *2 marks*

b Area = $0.5 \times 3 \times 4 = 6 \,cm^2$ *1 mark*

c Angle **A** = 53 degrees (*Allow up to 1 degree error each way.*) *1 mark*
Total 4 marks

Note to parent

The question requires the construction of a right-angled triangle. For this your child will use a ruler, pencil and angle measurer or set square. Try other constructions, e.g. a square with sides of 5 cm, a right-angled triangle with two sides of 5 cm. The formula given is used to calculate the area of the triangle. Additional questions you can try are:
1. Calculate the area of the smallest rectangle of card which could be used to make the gift box.
2. Calculate the area of waste cardboard when the gift box is produced from this rectangle.
3. Calculate the volume of the gift box.
You could also try to construct this gift box and similar ones from pieces of cardboard.

10 a Shape **D** (Shapes C and E have no base when folded.) *1 mark*
 b Shape **F** *1 mark*
 c Shape **G** *1 mark*
 d Shapes **C** and **E** *1 mark*
Total 4 marks

Note to parent

This question looks at a number of facets of Attainment Target 3: 'Shape, Space and Measures'.
It includes reference to folding a flat shape (net) to make a solid and tests knowledge of area and perimeter at a simple level.
The word *congruent* means that the shapes must be exactly the same with regard to side, length and angles. That is, one shape could fit exactly on top of the other.

11 a 514 and 154 *1 mark*
 b 415 and 145 *2 marks*
 c 8 *2 marks*
 d 324 or 576 *2 marks*
Total 7 marks

Note to parent

This question requires a knowledge of number properties such as whether they are even, square, are a multiple of, or have a particular factor.
Apart from awareness of even and odd numbers, which are introduced at Level 2, multiples, factors and square numbers are part of Levels 4 and 5.
A range of strategies can be used to solve parts of the question, but the ability to divide and multiply accurately while at the same time recognising whole number answers on the calculator, is important.

Test B Answers

12 a

GEMMA

Score	Count
2	5
4	3
6	4

SIMON

Score	Count
1	8
3	5
5	3

2 marks

12 b Gemma scored 46: (2 × 5) + (4 × 3) + (6 × 4)   *1 mark*
c (i) The game is **not** fair.   *1 mark*
  (ii) Odd and even numbers have an equal chance of occurring when a die is thrown but the total value of even numbers is greater than the total value of odd ones:
1 + 3 + 5 = 9
2 + 4 + 6 = 12   *1 mark*

Total 5 marks

Note to parent

This question tests children's knowledge of simple probability. They need to count the scores and enter the appropriate values in the frequency tables.

At this level, simple terms such as 'fair' and 'unfair', 'certain' and 'impossible' are expected to be used and understood. Games of chance are a good way of relating mathematical probability to children's everyday experience.

TEST TOTAL 55 MARKS

Test C Answers

TEST C *Pages 30–36*

1 a $\frac{1}{5}$ 20%   *1 mark*
  b 0.625   62.5%   *1 mark*
  c 0.8 $\frac{4}{5}$ *1 mark*
  Total 3 marks

Note to parent

This question tests knowledge of equivalence between fractions, decimals and percentages. Knowledge of equivalent fractions is further tested by asking for a fraction in its lowest form.

2 a One B box weighs 3 kg.   *1 mark*
  b 5C + 4 = 2C + 10   *1 mark*
  c One C box weighs 2 kg.   *1 mark*

Work out by 'trial and improvement' or, better, by 'balancing' and solving the equation.
5C − 2C + 4 = 10
       3C = 10 − 4
       3C = 6
        C = 2

Total 3 marks

Note to parent

Understanding of simple equations is best developed through visual examples and the basic idea of 'balancing'.

3 a

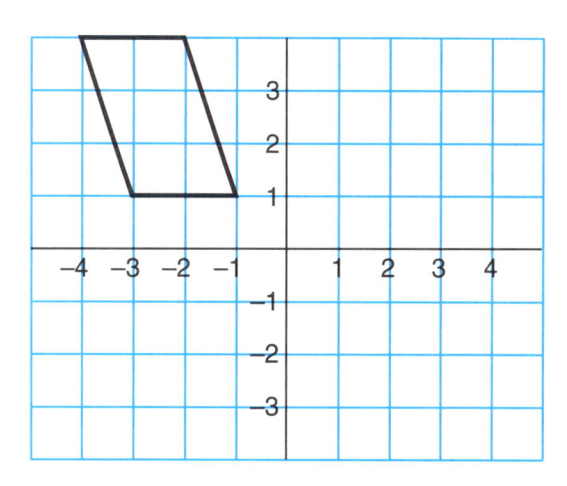

1 mark

49

Test C Answers

b [graph showing parallelogram with vertices at (1,1), (2,3), (3,3), (2,1) approximately in first quadrant]

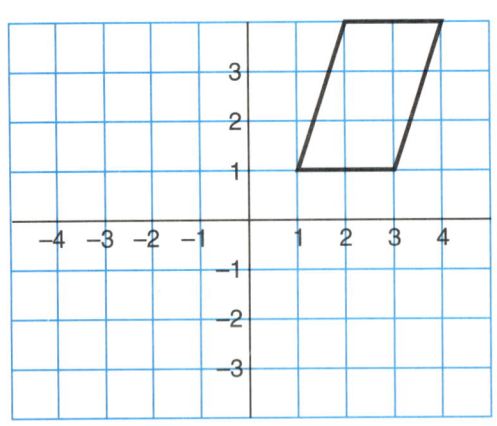

1 mark

c (1,1), (2,4), (4,4), (3,1) — *1 mark*
d Parallelogram (also accept quadrilateral) — *1 mark*

Total 4 marks

Note to parent

This question tests knowledge of co-ordinates in all four quadrants (i.e. including negative values) and the ability to transform a shape by reflection.

The mirror line for reflection is the *y* axis (*x* = 0)

4 a 10 — *1 mark*
 b Chance of 'No Score' = $\frac{2}{6}$ (or $\frac{1}{3}$) — *1 mark*

 c

	Die score					
Spinner score	1	2	3	4	5	6
0	1	2	3	4	5	6
0	1	2	3	4	5	6
1	2	3	4	5	6	7
2	3	4	5	6	7	8
3	4	5	6	7	8	9
4	5	6	7	8	9	10

There are 39 boxes to be completed. If your child scores 10–20 correctly award one mark; 21–29 award two marks; 30–39 award three marks. — *3 marks*

d Totals 5 and 6 occur most often. — *Both answers: 1 mark*
e $\frac{3}{36}$ (or $\frac{1}{12}$) — *1 mark*

Total 7 marks

Note to parent

Games of chance are often used to demonstrate mathematical probability. The chance of scoring any number on the spinner is $\frac{1}{6}$. It is the same on the six-sided die.

At Level 6, children are expected to combine events (spinner and a die) and list all possible events.

Test C Answers

5 a 32 children visit the museum. *1 mark*
25% represents 8 children.
100% will therefore give
$\frac{100}{25} \times 8 = 32$

b 4 children buy souvenirs. *1 mark*
12.5% represents $\frac{1}{8}$
$\frac{1}{8}$ of 32 = 4

c 75% of children take photographs. *1 mark*
$\frac{24}{32} \times 100 = 75$

Total 3 marks

Note to parent

At Level 6, children are expected to know which number represents 100% (see **a**) and to work out percentage values of totals in a range of problems.

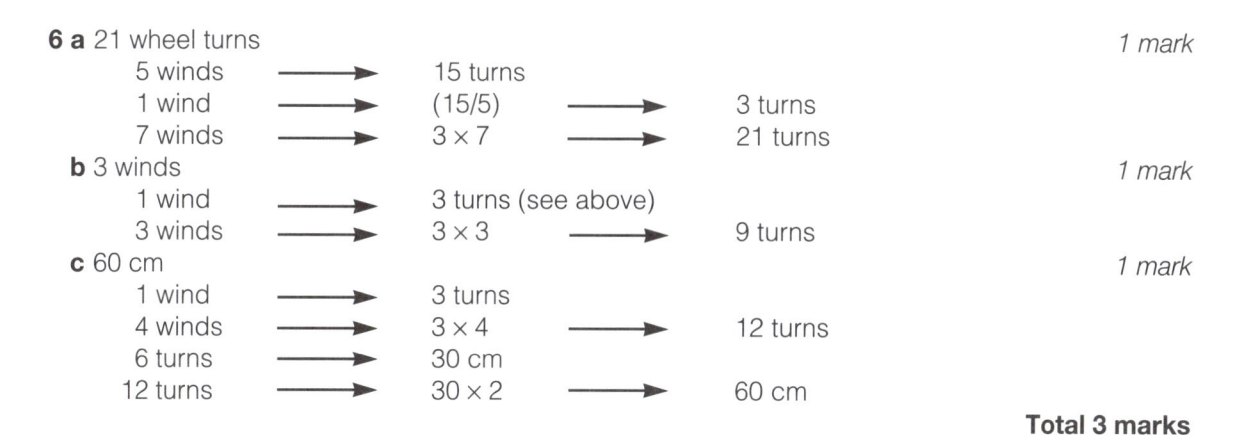

6 a 21 wheel turns *1 mark*
5 winds ⟶ 15 turns
1 wind ⟶ (15/5) ⟶ 3 turns
7 winds ⟶ 3 × 7 ⟶ 21 turns

b 3 winds *1 mark*
1 wind ⟶ 3 turns (see above)
3 winds ⟶ 3 × 3 ⟶ 9 turns

c 60 cm *1 mark*
1 wind ⟶ 3 turns
4 winds ⟶ 3 × 4 ⟶ 12 turns
6 turns ⟶ 30 cm
12 turns ⟶ 30 × 2 ⟶ 60 cm

Total 3 marks

Note to parent

This question is about ratio and direct proportion. The number of winds is directly connected to wheel turns.

Children can be introduced to this area of mathematics by looking at simple connections between two or more 'variables', e.g. total cost and number of chocolate bars.

Test C Answers

7 a Card used to make one box = 6200 cm² *2 marks*

(20 × 50) × 2 = 2000
(20 × 30) × 2 = 1200
(50 × 30) × 2 = 3000
‾‾‾‾
6200

b Area of the disc removed = 314 cm² *2 marks*
πr^2 = 3.14 × 10 × 10
    = 3.14 × 100
    = 314

Total 4 marks

Note to parent

The National Curriculum states that the children must understand and use formulae for calculating the areas of plane shapes, including circles at Level 6.

Your child needs to have met and used the formula Area = πr^2.

8 a
1 → 4
2 → 6
3 → 8
4 → 10
5 → 12

All correct: 1 mark

b 42 *1 mark*

c 'I double the number of white squares and add on two to give the number of blue squares' or something similar.
Also accept (w × 2 + 2) or the formula b = 2w + 2. *1 mark*

Total 3 marks

Note to parent

Children should learn to relate visual patterns to number patterns and also how to predict terms. They should begin to connect numbers using simple rules and formulae.

Test C Answers

9 a 8 cm

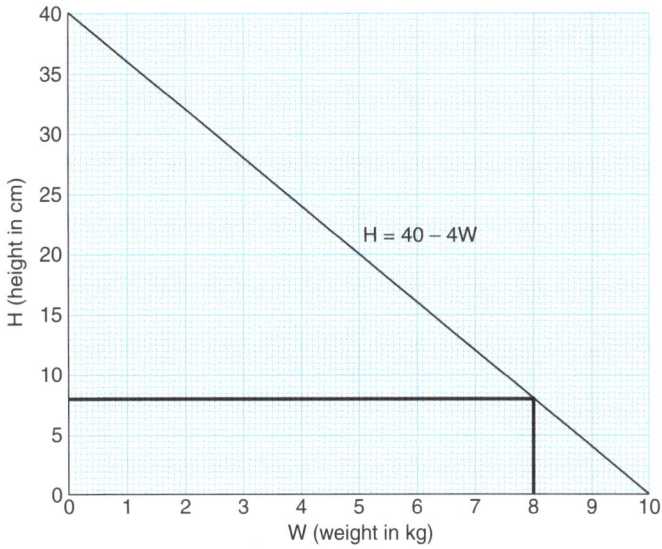

1 mark

b 6.25 kg (accept 6.2 kg or $6\frac{1}{4}$ kg)

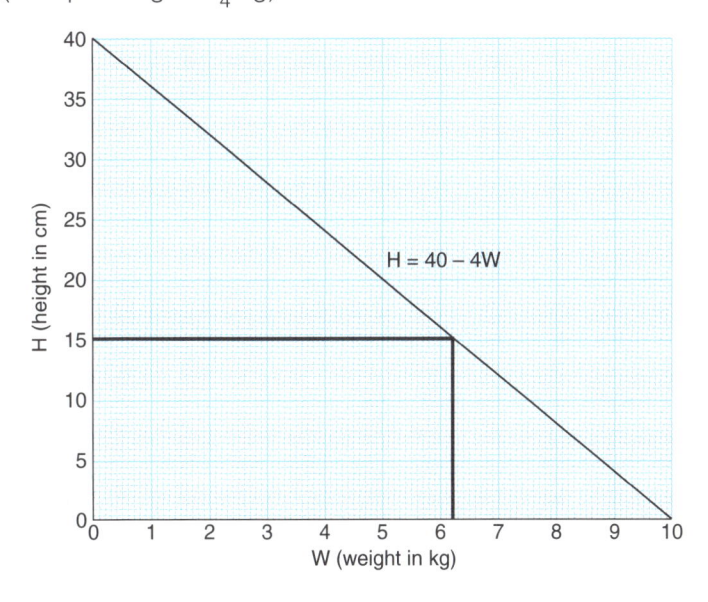

1 mark

c 10 kg

1 mark

Total 3 marks

Note to parent

Children need to be able to interpret information and algebraic relations presented as graphs. In this question, the connection between changing weights and height of the spring from the floor is represented as the continuous line on the graph.

This question also tests understanding of scales and the need to give a decimal answer read off the *x* axis.

TEST TOTAL 33 MARKS

Mental Arithmetic Answers

MENTAL ARITHMETIC *Page 37*

1. 12
2. 60
3. 55
4. 72
5. 33
6. 2p, 5p and 10p
7. 5203
8. 15
9. 9
10. 250
11. 4998
12. £2.30
13. 23
14. 350
15. 13
16. 19 degrees
17. 18
18. 0.75
19. 980
20. 31 or 37

Note to parent

This test is not going to be used in working out the level of your child. However, for guidance you might expect

- a child at Level 4 to score 9 out of 20
- a child at Level 5 to score 12 out of 20
- a child at Level 6 to score 16 out of 20

To help your child practise further, write out a list of similar questions and test him or her in the same way. It is also important to encourage children at Key Stage 2 to practise their multiplication tables often.

Mental Arithmetic Questions

INSTRUCTIONS FOR THE PARENT
Detach this page from the book. This test consists of twenty questions.

As you read these questions to your child, he or she should write the answers on the appropriate line on page 37.

Read out each question in turn, giving your child approximately 20 seconds to write down an answer. You can repeat the question if asked.

You should give no further help.

A CALCULATOR MUST NOT BE USED.

When the test is over, turn to page 54 to mark the test.

Award 1 mark for each correct answer.

THE QUESTIONS
1. Four multiplied by three.
2. Six multiplied by ten.
3. Thirty-three add twenty-two.
4. Eight multiplied by nine.
5. Fifty-seven take away twenty-four.
6. Which three coins make seventeen pence altogether?
7. Write down the number 'five thousand, two hundred and three'.
8. What is three-quarters of twenty?
9. What is fifty-four divided by six?
10. How many centimetres are there in two and a half metres?
11. Write down the figure which is two less than five thousand.
12. What is two pounds twenty-eight rounded to the nearest ten pence?
13. How many five pence coins are there in one pound fifteen?
14. How many days are there in fifty weeks?
15. If I was six years old five years ago, how old will I be two years from now?
16. By how much has the temperature dropped if it was seven degrees Celsius yesterday and is now minus twelve degrees?
17. If you square six and then halve it, what number will you have?
18. What is three-quarters as a decimal?
19. Multiply forty-nine by twenty.
20. Write down a prime number between thirty and forty.

Determining your child's level

FINDING YOUR CHILD'S LEVEL IN TESTS A AND B

When you have marked a test, enter the total number of marks your child scored for each question on the Marking Grid overleaf. Then add them up and enter the test total on the grid.

Using the total for each test, look at the chart below to determine your child's level for each test.

Test A or Test B

Level 2 or below	Level 3	Level 4	Level 5
up to 15	16–26	27–39	40+

FINDING YOUR CHILD'S OVERALL LEVEL IN MATHEMATICS

After you have worked out separate levels for Tests A and B, add up your child's total marks for the two tests. Use this total and the chart below to determine your child's overall level in Mathematics. The chart also shows you how your child's level in these tests compares with the target level for his or her age group.

Total for Tests A and B

Level 2 or below	Level 3	Level 4	Level 5
up to 31	32–53	54–79	80+
	Working towards target level for age group	Working at target level	Working beyond target level

If your child achieved Level 5 in Tests A and B, you may want to see how he or she does in Test C. A score of 20 or higher on Test C indicates that your child is working beyond the target level, at Level 6.

Marking Grid

TEST A — Pages 2–15

Question	Marks available	Marks scored	Question	Marks available	Marks scored
1	3		8	3	
2	3		9	4	
3	5		10	5	
4	3		11	8	
5	4		12	4	
6	5		13	4	
7	4		Total	55	

TEST B — Pages 16–29

Question	Marks available	Marks scored	Question	Marks available	Marks scored
1	4		7	7	
2	4		8	4	
3	4		9	4	
4	4		10	4	
5	4		11	7	
6	4		12	5	
			Total	55	

TEST C — Pages 30–36

Question	Marks available	Marks scored	Question	Marks available	Marks scored
1	3		6	3	
2	3		7	4	
3	4		8	3	
4	7		9	3	
5	3		Total	33	